Life On The Edge Of Faith

A Midweek Lenten Series

Beth Huener

CSS Publishing Company, Inc., Lima, Ohio

LIFE ON THE EDGE OF FAITH

For more information about CSS Publishing Company resources, visit our website at
www.csspub.com.

ISBN 0-7880-1790-X   PRINTED IN U.S.A.

*This series is
dedicated to the
Ecumenical Christian Community
of Monroeville, Ohio,
for whom and among whom,
it was originally developed.*

Table Of Contents

Introduction

Life On The Edge Of Faith is designed to increase and encourage lay involvement with one lay person reading the speech and another lay person leading the litanies and with the pastor preaching the sermon. This series is an ideal opportunity for the young people of the community to do everything but preach.

The speeches are only included in the five middle services. Most congregations focus on a more intentional ritual on Ash Wednesday (the imposition of ashes) and offer Holy Communion on Maundy Thursday. Liturgies for these rites are included and deal with the principal theme of the series: Life on the Edge of Faith.

The hymn which is included in every service, "Existing On The Edge Of Faith," may be sung to any Long Metre tune. Particularly fitting are "Distress," "Wareham," and "Waly, Waly," although "Duke Street," or "Old Hundred" will work.

Ash Wednesday

Life On The Edge Of Faith

Ash Wednesday Worship Service

The Opening Hymn

The Opening Litany   Jonah 2:2-9a
In my distress I called to the Lord,
  And he answered me.
From the depths of the grave I called for help,
  And you listened to my cry.
You hurled me into the deep,
  Into the very heart of the seas,
And the currents swirled about me;
  All your waves and breakers swept over me.
I said, "I have been banished from your sight;
  Yet I will look again toward your holy temple."
The engulfing waters threatened me, the deep surrounded me;
  Seaweed was wrapped around my head.
To the roots of the mountains I sank down;
  The earth beneath barred me in forever.
But you brought my life up from the pit,
  O Lord my God.
When my life was ebbing away,
  I remembered you, Lord.
And my prayer rose to you, to your holy temple.
  **Those who cling to worthless idols forfeit the grace that
  could be theirs.**
But I, with a song of thanksgiving,
  Will sacrifice to you.

The First Reading   Isaiah 58:1-12

9

The Imposition Of Ashes

Psalm 51:1-18 Stanza 1

Have mercy on me, O God, according to your unfailing love;
According to your great compassion blot out my transgressions.
Wash away all my iniquity and cleanse me from my sin.
For I know my transgressions, and my sin is always before me.
Against you, you only, have I sinned
And done what is evil in your sight,
So that you are proved right when you speak
And justified when you judge.
Surely I was sinful at birth,
Sinful from the time my mother conceived me.

The Confession Of Sins

Pastor:	Gracious and life-giving God, we stand before you knowing that without your authority in our lives, an authority which comes to us as gently as the sunshine and as suddenly and as powerfully as an earthquake and yet comes to us at every moment, lacking that present and omnipotent maintenance, we cease to exist. While this is so, still you stand before us with your hands outstretched, offering us your forgiveness.
All:	**Though we are unworthy, Lord, forgive us.**
Right Side:	**When we fail to bring your love into consideration or when we slip into apathy or despair about the world,**
Left side:	**When we fail to take strength and courage from the example of your Son,**
All:	**Though we are unworthy, Lord, forgive us.**
Right Side:	**When, by our inaction, we allow justice, greed, selfishness, and even cruelty to go unchecked,**
Left Side:	**When by our inaction, we allow your truth to go unspoken and undefended, ignored and mocked,**

10

All:	**Though we are unworthy, Lord, forgive us.**
Right Side:	**When with our apathy and despair, we fall into dangerous, abusive, and destructive habits,**
Left Side:	**Or allow our hopelessness to turn into cynicism or into the deadly desire for power, wealth, or other forms of earthly corruptible security,**
All:	**Though we are unworthy, Lord, forgive us.**
Right Side:	**When in our weakness and fear, we allow ourselves to be dragged down into a place in which we see no way to live which does not involve sinful behavior,**
Left Side:	**And perhaps find our strength and our courage in sin instead of your goodness,**
All:	**Though we are unworthy, Lord, forgive us.**
Right Side:	**When we find profane power and treacherous security in acts of injustice, greed, selfishness, and cruelty,**
Left Side:	**And allow others to pay the cost for that power and security,**
All:	**Though we are unworthy, Lord, forgive us.**
Right Side:	**When we neglect the truth that your Son died to show us, and when, with our fearful doubt and our lack of support, we abuse those who try to spread that truth with words and actions,**
Left Side:	**When we show the world how little your love really means to us,**
All:	**Though we are unworthy, Lord, forgive us.**
Pastor:	We lay our lives, unworthy of even a glance from you, at your feet and beg you for mercy, not because of anything we have done or can hope to do, but because of your Son's sacrifice that paid our debt.
People:	**Humbly, we give you thanks. Amen.**

Psalm 51   Stanza 2

Surely you desire truth in the inner parts;
   You teach me wisdom in the inmost place.

11

Cleanse me with hyssop, and I will be clean;
Wash me, and I will be whiter than snow.
Let me hear joy and gladness;
Let the bones you have crushed rejoice.
Hide your face from my sins
And blot out all my iniquity.
Create in me a pure heart, O God,
And renew a steadfast spirit within me.
Do not cast me from your presence
Or take your Holy Spirit from me.
Restore to me the joy of your salvation
And grant me a willing spirit, to sustain me.

The Second Lesson   2 Corinthians 5:20b—6:10

The Gospel Verse   Matthew 6:19-21
Pastor: Do not store up for yourselves treasures on earth, where
moth and rust destroy, and where thieves break in and
steal. But store up for yourselves treasures in heaven,
where moth and rust do not destroy, and where thieves
do not break in and steal.
People: **For where your treasure is, there your heart will be
also.**

The Gospel Lesson   Luke 18:9-14

The Sermon Hymn   "Existing On The Edge Of Faith"
Existing on the edge of faith,
Christ's promised peace alone we seek
Grant us the strength to look at you,
We fear our lives are frail and weak.

Your gift of faith fills us with hope
That life can be forever bright
But faced with this world's hungry lies,
We feel our hearts lose your love's light.

12

Teach us the humble road to walk.
Open our hearts to your embrace
Then we can show the world your love,
With acts of mercy, joy, and grace.

The Sermon

The Prayers Of The People

Pastor: Dear Lord, grant to all who come before you this night, the peace of your presence. We do not pray this so that you will do it, for you are ever present. We pray that all who invoke your presence will feel its warmth in spite of the coldness of the world, will see it shining through even the brightest, fleeting glitter of our misdirected hopes, and will hear it above the traffic of our desires which continually roars in our ears. Our heads deeply bowed,

People: **We pray to you, O Lord.**

Pastor: Draw us more deeply, Lord, into the faith that can be ours through your Holy Spirit. Remind us that sins which keep us from embracing that faith have been rendered harmless by the crucifixion and resurrection of your Son. Surround our lives with your loving presence, Holy God, Three in One, so that neither fear nor loneliness can invade our lives and lead us from you. Our heads deeply bowed,

People: **We pray to you, O Lord.**

Pastor: During these next six weeks. Lord, help us to repent of our distance from you, distances which we have allowed, not only because of fear or loneliness, but because of selfishness and laziness as well. Teach us to feel the dread of that distance so that we feel the joy of your nearness. Our heads deeply bowed,

People: **We pray to you, O Lord.**

Pastor: We thank you, Lord, because you have promised that you will be with your creation this night, that you will comfort the fearful, strengthen the weak, be present to

13

the lonely, and encourage the faithful. Help us to work to be your hands and feet in and among your people. Our heads deeply bowed,

People: **We pray to you, O Lord.**

Pastor: Standing on the edge of faith, we beg you to hold us up, dear Lord, with your gift of peace and hear our prayers.

People: **Amen.**

The Offering

The Word Of Institution For Ash Wednesday

Pastor: Great God in Heaven, you sent your Son to take on our condition and, being sinless, to die for our sin. Raising him from death, you sent your Spirit to help us to understand things that are too beautiful for us to see. We give you thanks for these beautiful and incomprehensible things that conquer our fear and free us for service. Break us from our chains, Lord, and bind us to your will, the will your Son so humbly obeyed.

People: **At his invitation, we pray. Amen.**

The Words Of Institution

The Lord's Prayer

The Prayer After Communion

Pastor: We give you thanks, Lord, that you have welcomed us, unworthy as we are, into your presence. Fill us with a gratitude born of the knowledge of your Son's sacrifice and send us forth to embrace the freedom and joy this sacrifice brings.

People: **Amen.**

The Closing Hymn

Ash Wednesday Sermon

I don't know how many times I have heard cancer patients say that they don't have the time for chemotherapy or radiation. Of course, I have come to believe that what they are usually feeling when they say that they don't have time for chemotherapy is the same thing that most of us are feeling when we say we don't have time for something and that is that we don't want to do it. And what is the reason most of us don't want to do things? We are afraid, pure and simple. We are even afraid of doing things when the repercussions of not doing them are more fearsome. It would be easier not to make room in our lives for that extra self-discipline or generosity or maturity or courage. If we ignore the cure long enough, maybe the problem will disappear.

Whoever said that the behavior of human beings, especially frightened human beings, made sense? The behavior of the Pharisee probably made sense to him. And up to a point, it can honestly be viewed as making sense, even spiritually. No matter what else you say about the Pharisee, you have to admit that he is thanking God for his good character, and, as far as the activity he uses as an example of his character, this might be called over and above the call of duty. Only the tithing of crops was required. This man tithed all he received, not just crops. And the kind of fasting he did was practiced only by the most zealous Jews.

So this was a fairly impressive person, and I wonder if his prayer was not in earnest. He certainly did have reason to be grateful and he was indeed understanding correctly where he should be sending his gratitude. Gratitude does sweeten our joy and fill us with contentment that we can obtain nowhere else. Other Pharisees have been known to pray prayers like this; it seems that many of them were given to comparisons as this Pharisee was. Around 70 A.D., a rabbi wrote, "I thank thee, O Lord, my God, that thou hast given me a place among those who sit in the House of Study, and not among those who sit at the street corners; for I rise early and they rise early but I rise early to study the word of the law and they rise

15

early to engage in vain things; I labor and they labor, but I labor and receive a reward and they labor and receive no reward."

That leads me to my only question with regard to this Pharisee's prayer: What was his reward? His joy was made sweeter and his contentment was enhanced, but from where I sit it seems to me that both his joy and his contentment were already hale and hearty. His prayer was not like that of the tax collector. But it wouldn't be, would it? I am wondering how the tax collector even made it into the temple without being attacked and thrown out of the temple area. As a Roman collaborator and tax collector, he fed off his community the same way that welfare cheats and drug dealers feed off of ours today. Make no mistake. The Pharisee was being generous even to be in the same temple with him. But this man has been blessed because he is not looking for a reward, whereas the Pharisee has managed to convince himself that he needs nothing from God, not even forgiveness. The tax collector, having no such luxury, has no such barrier to his reward. He is eager, no, he is desperate, to plunge the spade of his prayer into the filth of his sin and dig a hole for grace to fill. He knows of his sickness and he has stripped his soul bare to receive the painful but life-renewing medicine of forgiveness. This evening, we begin our dark journey into our own sinfulness, so that with the knowledge of our need, we will greet, with gratitude, the one who, with his blood, fills it.

Ash Wednesday Notes

Traditionally, the ashes are made by burning the palms used the previous Passion Sunday and mixed with enough oil to make a paste, although any ash may be used.

Those who wish to receive the imposition of ashes come forward and the minister draws a cross on their foreheads with the ashes, saying, "Remember you are dust, and to dust you will return. Turn from sin and be faithful to the gospel."

If there is no imposition of ashes, the Old Testament Lesson is Joel 2:1-2, 12-17 in place of the Isaiah reading.

For the confession of sins, the responsive parts may be men, right side and left side, or another such division.

Life On The Edge Of Faith

A Sleeping Disciple

The Opening Speech

The Opening Hymn

The Dialogue   Habakkuk 2:1-3
I will stand at my watch
And station myself on the ramparts;
I will look to see what he will say to me,
And what answer I am to give to this complaint.
Then the Lord replied: "Write down the revelation
**And make it plain on tablets so that a herald may run
with it.**
For the revelation awaits an appointed time;
It speaks of the end and will not prove false.
Though it linger, wait for it;
It will certainly come and will not delay."

The Old Testament Lesson   1 Kings 19:1-8

Psalm 121   Stanza 1
I lift up my eyes to the hills
Where does my help come from?
My help comes from the Lord,
The Maker of heaven and earth.
He will not let your foot slip
He who watches over you will not slumber;
Indeed, he who watches over Israel
Will neither slumber nor sleep.

The Gospel Verse   Matthew 6:19-21

Pastor: Do not store up for yourselves treasures on earth, where
moth and rust destroy, and where thieves break in and
steal. But store up for yourselves treasures in heaven,
where moth and rust do not destroy, and where thieves
do not break in and steal.

People: **For where your treasure is, there your heart will be
also.**

The Gospel   Matthew 26:36-56

The Sermon Hymn   "Existing On The Edge of Faith"
Existing on the edge of faith,
Christ's promised peace alone we seek
Grant us the strength to look to you,
We fear our lives are frail and weak.

We dare not trust our feeble strength
When we our Lord seek to obey
Soothe, loving Lord, our anxious hearts.
Our fragile spirits often stray.

Teach us the humble road to walk.
Open our hearts to your embrace
Then we can show the world your love,
With acts of mercy, joy, and grace.

The Sermon

Psalm 121   Stanza 2
The Lord watches over you
   The Lord is your shade at your right hand;
The sun will not harm you by day,
   Nor the moon by night.
The Lord will keep you from all harm
   He will watch over your life;
The Lord will watch over your coming and going
   Both now and forevermore.

The Offering

The Prayers Of The People

Pastor: Let us pray to be made brave and vigilant witnesses for our Redeemer.

Dear heavenly Father, you know better than we do that without your help we are far from equal to the enormous task and precious privilege you have placed before us. You have already made available all that we need to pursue your will with joy and courage. Teach us, Lord, to embrace those living tools. Watchfully waiting,

People: **We pray to you, O Lord.**

Pastor: Help us to reach out to each other for strength and encouragement. By means of your gift to us of faith, teach us to place faith in each other. Keep us from the temptation to compete with one another in pursuit of any other purpose outside of serving you. In so doing, teach us to rejoice in all the victories your people achieve in your name. Watchfully waiting,

People: **We pray to you, O Lord.**

Pastor: Keep us aware of all of the opportunities of service that are around us constantly in the lonely, suffering, and confused lives of the people with whom we come into contact. Take away the fear of embarrassment or rejection and fill us with the joy of witnessing. Watchfully waiting,

People: **We pray to you, O Lord.**

(Other petitions may be offered)

Pastor: Standing on the edge of faith, we beg you to hold us up, dear Lord, with your gift of peace and hear our prayers.

People: **Amen.**

The Lord's Prayer

The Benediction

Pastor: May God himself, the God of peace, sanctify you through and through. May your whole spirit, soul, and body be kept blameless at the coming of our Lord Jesus Christ.

People: **He who calls you is faithful and he will do it.**

The Closing Hymn

Opening Speech: A Sleeping Disciple

I don't know why I could not keep my eyes open. Sure, it was getting to be a long day, but we'd certainly had long days before. I really should have been wide awake. Since it was so near the time of Passover, there were Roman soldiers all over the place. This made everybody nervous, so you could tell that something, somewhere was going to blow. So instead of being sleepy, I should have been wide awake.

The only explanation I can find is the fact that I have always found his presence very tiring. No, not tiring, exciting. No, not tiring really. It's just that every day, it seems I am doing something else I never dreamed I'd be doing. I remember the first time he sent us out on our own. I remember feeling like I was the only person on the planet that had ever felt the way I was feeling. But, boy, when we all joined back up with him, I was really tired. We were about to go up to the hills to rest, but, just before we were about to leave, another huge crowd showed up. Well, I might have been angry, but I wasn't. Jesus must be rubbing off on me. One thing about Jesus, he always had patience. We stayed and worked among those people for another four hours. It was then that some of us got worried. We knew that we were out in the middle of nowhere. As ridiculous as it seems now, we were beginning to be impatient with Jesus. We were really worried that Jesus was behaving irresponsibly. What an idea! Jesus wasn't worried. He knew what he was going to do. He fed all of those people on a few scraps of food, with some left over for us.

As I say, it is exciting. In fact, when Jesus isn't around, everything else seems deadly dull and there's little better to do than go to sleep. But it still doesn't explain why on that night, of all nights, the night my Lord needed me the most, I was too sleepy to stay awake with him. In my half-awake, half-asleep state, I could hear him about a stone's throw away from us, moaning as though his whole being had turned against him. But still, I couldn't stay awake.

But we were wide awake soon enough. He had just returned to where we were all sacked out. That's one good thing — at least I

21

wasn't the only one. Anyway, nobody had a chance to make excuses or apologize before the guards came. Some of the guys said that they'd expected it for a long time. Some of them had even said that Jesus was going too far, that he was making the religious leaders nervous, that he was placing Israel's position in the Roman constellation at risk. So I guess we shouldn't have been that surprised when Jesus was arrested. We were all so scared, but he was even calmer than usual, if that's possible. And because of that I felt less and less worthy of his companionship, so I just ran. But now that he rose, just as he said he would, I don't think I will ever run or fall asleep on the watch again.

Lent 1 Sermon

There is a story about a man who could not climb out of a well even though he was standing just a few inches below the end of a rope. Ordinarily, this might sound extraordinary. However, it ceases to be so when one realizes that this is a man who never looked up even on the good days when the sky was blue and the sun was shining and the birds were singing. Whether out of habit or insecurity or foul temperment, he never looked up. One has to wonder what good his consistent focus on the ground did him when he fell into the well anyway. But such he did. And he screamed himself nearly hoarse for help, but still, he didn't look up. When a child finally did hear him and look down the well, he did finally look up. That is when he saw the rope.

Perhaps the disciples who slept while their Lord suffered were unwilling to look up as well. Whether because of habit or insecurity or perhaps even foul temperment, it seems that their focus was very close to the ground, that they were incapable of expecting or imagining anything they had not expected or imagined before. And honestly, were we to try to put ourselves in their position, it would be easy enough for us to understand why they had such difficulty. After all, in most cases, dead is dead. More to the point, in most cases, power is power and in the first century in Israel, the power was held by Rome and those who were willing to do homage to it. It was not held by a man from the North Country with few advantages and no education. Power that came from armies and political clout could be expected to follow through with its threats. Power that came from words of love and acts of kindness, as miraculous as they may seem, could not necessarily be expected to follow through with its promises. And the longer we look at this power issue that exists today as powerfully as it did those long years ago, the less the question seems to be one of power, or even of plausibility. It seems that the real question is one of motive.

When you really get right down to it, the disciples did not fear the Romans more than they trusted Jesus because the Romans had more power and they could understand the source of that power.

Nor did they trust Jesus less than they feared the Romans because they could not understand the source of his power. For the people of first century Jerusalem, the problem with Jesus is that he did not seem to gain anything by doing what he did.

Self-sacrifice is all right every once in a while, but with Jesus it was a steady theme. Not only did it confuse the disciples, it probably left them feeling that to emulate him would be impossible. That was until they realized that what Jesus wanted, they needed. The teaching, the living, the healing, and the bleeding and dying were part of his mission on earth, but we all received what we needed when, by means of his resurrection, God ended death's power over us.

Now we know where that power comes from and we can see clearly that it comes from a source that is not like armies or political power, which, while they may seem awesome, can be destroyed or dissolved in a day. Not only is our Lord's power a power that will never be destroyed or dissolved, it is a power which lifts our heads up out of our self-imposed weariness and gloom and gives us the joy to expect what we could not have otherwise imagined: our belonging to God forever.

Life On The Edge Of Faith

The High Priest

The Opening Speech

The Opening Hymn

The Dialogue   Isaiah 56:1-5
Maintain justice and do what is right,
> **For my salvation is close at hand and my righteousness will soon be revealed.**

Blessed is the man who does this,
> **The man who holds it fast,**

Who keeps the Sabbath without desecrating it,
> **And keeps his hand from doing any evil.**

Let no foreigner who has bound himself to the Lord say,
> **"The Lord will surely exclude me from his people."**

And let not any eunuch complain,
> **"I am only a dry tree."**

For this is what the Lord says:
> **"To the eunuchs who keep my Sabbaths,**

Who choose what pleases me and hold fast to my covenant —
> **To them I will give within my temple**

And its walls a memorial and a name better than sons and daughters;
> **I will give them an everlasting name that will not be cut off."**

The Old Testament Lesson   Exodus 32:1-14

Psalm 77:11-20   Stanza 1
I will remember the deeds of the Lord;
> **Yes, I will remember your miracles of long ago.**

25

I will meditate on all your works
And consider all your mighty deeds.
Your ways, O God, are holy.
What god is so great as our God?
You are the God who performs miracles;
You display your power among the peoples.
With your mighty arm you redeemed your people,
The descendants of Jacob and Joseph.

The Gospel Verse   Matthew 6:19-21
Pastor: Do not store up for yourselves treasures on earth, where
moth and rust destroy, and where thieves break in and
steal. But store up for yourselves treasures in heaven,
where moth and rust do not destroy, and where thieves
do not break in and steal.
People: **For where your treasure is, there your heart will be
also.**

The Gospel   Matthew 26:57-68

The Sermon

The Sermon Hymn   "Existing On The Edge Of Faith"
Existing on the edge of faith,
Christ's promised peace alone we seek
Grant us the strength to look to you,
We fear our lives are frail and weak.

For those who trust your mercy, Lord,
Great joy is found at every turn.
Help us to bring this to each task,
When thwarted, we for justice yearn.

Teach us the humble road to walk.
Open our hearts to your embrace
Then we can show the world your love,
With acts of mercy, joy, and grace.

26

Psalm 77:11-20 Stanza 2

The waters saw you, O God, the waters saw you and writhed;
The very depths were convulsed.
The clouds poured down water, the skies resounded with thunder;
Your arrows flashed back and forth.
Your thunder was heard in the whirlwind, your lightning lit up the world;
The earth trembled and quaked.
Your path led through the sea,
Your way through the mighty waters though your footprints were not seen.
You led your people like a flock
By the hand of Moses and Aaron.

The Offering

The Prayers Of The People

Pastor: Let us pray to recognize and rejoice in the loving gift of faith that God has for us.

Father in heaven, far beyond our understanding, you reach your loving hand toward us. We ask that you help us to grasp the wonder of this love and the freedom such faith gives us. Doing this, we will not be able to restrain the joyful witness that will pour out from us. Claiming for ourselves the gifts you have for us,

People: **We pray to you, O Lord.**

Pastor: Forgive us, Lord, for hiding behind the world you have given us and claiming the things of this world which are destined for extinction and even the relationships you have given us as the gods on which we rely. Increase in us the knowledge of your love, thereby increasing our peace of mind and heart. Claiming for ourselves the gifts you have for us,

People: **We pray to you, O Lord.**

Pastor: Increase in us, dear Lord, the knowledge of your will and the dedication we feel to the proclamation of your good news. Unite your church so that the world with which you have blessed us may see the powerful force of your love. Claiming for ourselves the gifts you have for us,

People: **We pray to you, O Lord.**

Pastor: Standing on the edge of faith, we beg you to hold us up, dear Lord, with your gift of peace and hear our prayers.

People: **Amen.**

The Lord's Prayer

The Benediction   1 Thessalonians 5:23-24

Pastor: May God himself, the God of peace, sanctify you through and through. May your whole spirit, soul, and body be kept blameless at the coming of our Lord Jesus Christ.

People: **He who calls you is faithful and he will do it.**

The Closing Hymn

Opening Speech: The High Priest

You'd think I would be past all of this. After all, if a person is the high priest, he should be able to make an assessment and stick by it, and usually I can, but not this time.

All the way around, this time was different. I didn't think so at first. He seemed like just another troublemaker. He had all the characteristics: the ability to attract the big crowds with the flashy miracles, the charismatic personality. People I trust kept telling me that there was more to this one. But I figured it was just wishful thinking. After all, people had started to claim that he was the Messiah finally come. Who wouldn't want to believe that? But, I'm afraid that for those of us who just barely manage to believe in the promise of the coming Messiah at all, it's a bit of a stretch to imagine that God would send his Anointed One in the person of a poor, ignorant man from the hill country, or into this traitorous generation.

I gave him the benefit of the doubt, though. Even more than that, for one fleeting moment I let myself wonder. And I have to tell you, for that one moment, I felt like my world was turning upside down. I don't even think it had as much to do with the fact that I wanted to believe in him as it had to do with the amount of energy I had expended with regard to him.

You see, I have never condoned murder of any kind in my whole life. But, you'd really have to understand what we've been up against here. We have been striving to live as faithful Jews in a country in which striving to live as a faithful Jew is considered a waste of time because it doesn't get you anywhere with Rome. So all we have tried to do is strike a happy medium. We have continued to obey our God, despite the consequences to our income level, our social prestige, and even our personal safety. We have known that in order to continue God's work, we would need to keep from causing Rome trouble. Not that they care who or what we worship, they just want the tax money to keep flowing. And, of course, this is something that this country rube, this Jesus person was not sophisticated enough to understand. And as I say, I am not one to ever condone murder, but we gave this guy warning after warning. For three years, we asked him to watch what he said, to keep from undermining the elders and the priests, to stop giving Rome ammunition, but he would not listen. He continued to threaten our already shaky relationship with Rome.

So, it came down to a choice — either we shut him up, or we let Rome shut the synagogues down. And that was no choice. In the face of our sacred duty, to prevent the death of 2,000 years of devotion, of tradition, of remembrance, one life seemed a small price to be paid. The price didn't feel small that night. I found myself hoping that he was the Messiah. I almost begged him to say that he was. But he just stood there. When he finally did speak, it didn't make any sense. And in that moment, I felt my faith in the coming Messiah vanish. But I still wish I could be sure I didn't send God's Anointed One to his shameful death.

Lent 2 Sermon

The story of the high priest reminds us that faith is a frightening thing. It insists that we abandon our reliance on that which makes sense, on that which we can measure and reasonably predict. It is a paradox that we would rather depend on a world which, time and time again, assures us that it will eventually destroy itself than a God that assures us that faith in him is the only path to safety from the predictability of self-destruction. The Chief Priest behaves in the text that we have before us today as though he was almost literally hanging between hope and despair, faith and doubt. But it is clear that at least at this moment, he chooses that which he considers more reliable: the world he can perceive with his senses and about which he is therefore prepared to make a judgment.

As rational as this decision may seem, it defies reality as people perceive it day after day. When people make the decision to reject the possibility of the hope of redemption through the Son of God, they are using the same logic that people use when they reject the possibility of love, the possibility of love the way God intended, a love that trusts and allows the ones embracing it to reveal their strengths and weaknesses and to cease being afraid to ask for what they need. People do reject the opportunity to be sustained and comforted by this gift of love all the time, even people in the established relationships of marriage and family.

When we doubt the gift of faith that God has given to us, we are treating God the same way that we treat the people we love when we refuse to trust them. We do this even though we know the advantages of trusting those we love and we know the advantages of trusting God, but still we consider, beyond all good sense, the advantage of the upper hand to be more desirable than trusting cooperation.

There is a story about the creation of the world. When it came time for the creation of cats, Lucretia, Queen of Cats, stood before God. She told her maker that on the face of earth, cats would be humanity's humble servant. They would come when called, be loving and obedient, and never, ever scratch their masters. From his

31

throne, the creator of the world said, "No. You will ignore, distrust, and resist your human masters. You will not come when called. And when they try to show you their love, you will hold it in contempt and when they get too close, you will scratch. In this way, the human will see how they treat me."

We are behaving as irrationally as a cat that scratches its owner, the one who feeds and protects it, when we reject the gift of faith that God gives to us. And just as people in the established relationships of marriage and family often fail to trust and rely on each other and therefore threaten the relationship, people living in the context of faith often fail to trust and rely on God and, in so doing, jeopardize their relationship with God. We call that sin, but we also call it rejection, not just of God, but of the possibility of hope.

As rational as the high priest may have seemed, he rejected the one thing that could have made him happy. Who knows? The Gospel according to Saint Matthew only privileges us with a tiny sliver of this man's experience. Perhaps, after he saw what all the world would shortly see, he became greedy for the gift God holds out for us all.

Life On The Edge Of Faith

A Maid

The Opening Speech

The Opening Hymn

The Dialogue   Jeremiah 14:7-9

Although our sins testify against us, O Lord,
> **Do something for the sake of your name.**

For our backsliding is great;
> **We have sinned against you.**

O Hope of Israel, its Savior in times of distress,
> **Why are you like a stranger in the land, like a traveler who stays only a night?**

Why are you like a man taken by surprise,
> **Like a warrior powerless to save?**

You are among us, O Lord, and we bear your name;
> **Do not forsake us!**

The Old Testament Lesson   Deuteronomy 7:12-16

Psalm 119 (33-37)   Stanza 1

Teach me, O Lord, to follow your decrees;
> **Then I will keep them to the end.**

Give me understanding,
> **And I will keep your law and obey it with all my heart.**

Direct me in the path of your commands,
> **For there I find delight.**

Turn my heart toward your statutes
> **And not toward selfish gain.**

The Gospel Verse   Matthew 6:19-21

Pastor: Do not store up for yourselves treasures on earth, where
               moth and rust destroy, and where thieves break in and
               steal. But store up for yourselves treasures in heaven,
               where moth and rust do not destroy, and where thieves
               do not break in and steal.

People: **For where your treasure is, there your heart will be
               also.**

The Gospel   Matthew 26:69-75

The Sermon Hymn   "Existing On The Edge Of Faith"
    Existing on the edge of faith,
    Christ's promised peace alone we seek
    Grant us the strength to look to you,
    We fear our lives are frail and weak.

    Like a high wall, our sinful hearts
    Stand in the way of your embrace
    With gentle hands you bear us up
    To see your all forgiving face.

    Teach us the humble road to walk.
    Open our hearts to your embrace
    Then we can show the world your love,
    With acts of mercy, joy, and grace.

The Sermon

Psalm 119 (37-40)   Stanza 2
    Turn my eyes away from worthless things;
        Preserve my life according to your word.
    Fulfill your promise to your servant,
        So that you may be feared.
    Take away the disgrace I dread,
        For your laws are good.
    How I long for your precepts!
        Preserve my life in your righteousness.

The Offering

The Prayers Of The People

Pastor: Let us pray to be representatives of God's grace in our lives.

Lord God, you alone know the loneliness we suffer when we feel estranged from you. Keep us aware of how our words and actions lead us away from you and how they also may keep others from a more complete knowledge of your love. Seeking to be faithful to you,

People: **We pray to you, O Lord.**

Pastor: Straighten the path before us Lord, so that we can know your will. So often, we forget that you sent your Son to do just that. Help us to open our eyes to the knowledge he died to give us. Help us to remember that the roadblocks of sin, selfishness, and rage have been moved out of the way by his sacrifice for us. Seeking to be faithful to you,

People: **We pray to you, O Lord.**

Pastor: Give us the joy that can only come from placing our hope in the only future of which we can be assured. Keep us from placing our faith in things which give us only the illusion of control but promise only that they, like all other earthly defenders, will one day abandon us. Shelter us in your stronghold, Lord. Seeking to be faithful to you,

People: **We pray to you, O Lord.**

Pastor: Standing on the edge of faith, we beg you to hold us up, dear Lord, with your gift of peace and hear our prayers.

People: **Amen.**

The Lord's Prayer

The Benediction   1 Thessalonians 5:23-24

Pastor: May God himself, the God of peace, sanctify you through
and through. May your whole spirit, soul, and body be
kept blameless at the coming of our Lord Jesus Christ.

People: **He who calls you is faithful and he will do it.**

The Closing Hymn

Opening Speech: A Maid

I knew he was one of them. I knew it from the country way he talked. After you have worked downtown as long as I have and have waited on as many tables as I have, once people start talking, you know exactly where they come from. That's why it was such a joke that this big clown pretended he had never even met this Jesus character. You know, the one who was telling everybody he was going to destroy the temple and rebuild it in three days. I mean, give me a break. The population of the hill country must be tiny. How many people would want to live up there in the mountains anyway? With a character like that hanging around, everybody's going to know him.

Yeah, that guy was a real clown. Got all excited when he thought he was going to be found out. Started to swear up and down that he'd never laid eyes on him. Showed his true colors, now, didn't he? I guess that's what bugs me most about these "holier than thou" types. They talk tough as long as everything is going their way, but put a little heat under them and they'll say whatever they think you want to hear. But, I guess I have to give the dude credit. Probably most of the rest of this Jesus guy's followers took off back into the hills. I don't know for sure but this guy is the only one I've seen the last couple of days when only last week they were as thick as hair on a dog, waving palm branches and hooting and hollering. I mean, where did they all go? Total bail out, man.

You know, I may not be perfect, but I'm no hypocrite, not like these apostles or whatever they're calling themselves. You do the best you can, and since you know that eventually you're going to mess up, you don't try to tell anyone else what to do. It's a lot safer that way. I know that there have to be people who tell us how to lead good lives. I suppose that is the reason for all temple nonsense. When these priests do something bad, they go and buy themselves a couple of birds and offer them to God, I guess. Boy, in my case I would be buying birds every half hour. I guess it's a good thing I'm not a priest. I'd keep the temple merchants in business. It seems an awful silly way to live your life, though. I mean, what if you did something wrong and you forgot about it because you got away with it, or if you didn't even know you had done it because the person you messed with never told you about it. What about that? You wouldn't go and offer a sacrifice so God wouldn't forgive you. Like I say, strange way to live your life. Running back to the temple all the time.

No wonder the big wigs were freaking out about this guy. He said he was going to tear down the temple. I don't know. That guy said some things that really shook up the stuffed shirts. Like loving and forgiving your enemies. But I never saw them any angrier than when he kicked out all the temple merchants. How were all the holy people going to be forgiven now that they can't make their sacrifices? I wonder if that's what he meant when he said he was giving his life as a sacrifice for many. I wonder if that "many" includes me?

Lent 3 Sermon

In *The Plague*, a strange and allegorical novel by Albert Camus, the city of Onan on the coast of North Africa is sealed off from the rest of the world as a result of a freak but virulent outbreak of the bubonic plague. But, it seems there is no bad wind that does not blow someone some good fortune. Cottage industries popped up all over the city. Anyone with a boat began to sell people black market tickets to Europe, promising to get them there in short order. At least one of these new entrepreneurs had no intention of taking these people anywhere. After being charged an exorbitant fee, his customers were told to wait in a warehouse for the boat, which of course never came. Once the plague ended, they left the warehouse. Their extortionists had no reason to fear that they would tell the authorities of their misdeeds because their pursuing transport out of the city was itself illegal.

It seems that our society is becoming more like a society under siege. This kind of behavior is becoming more and more prevalent as honest citizens refuse to run for office for the common good and as brave, strong women abandon careers in the military because of the way they fear they will be treated. Self-care becomes paramount in the face of the cold, inhospitable climate of public cynicism and distrust. So, just like Peter, people give in to the temptation of self-protection at the world's expense.

Temptation is the attraction of a lesser good which causes us to reject, ignore, or postpone a greater good. It is its most powerful when we are not truly caring for ourselves, when we are not trusting God. Oddly enough, it is its most deceptive when we catch ourselves saying something like, "I have to take care of myself, too." Probably Peter did not even articulate these words in his mind, but they were present enough to do him damage. I wonder how many people in Onan said that to themselves while they were trying to resist the temptation to escape that plague-gripped city even if it did mean breaking the law. By illegally attempting to escape the city, these people were not just breaking the law, they were abandoning their fellow citizens in distress and possibly carrying a disastrous infection into a more heavily populated part of the world. From even a humanistic point of view, by abandoning their community and by disregarding the safety of other human beings, they were not caring for themselves. Eventually, they would find themselves in need of other people with whom they have not maintained a relationship. From a Christian point of view, their attempted escape from a community in pain is even more selfish and foolhardy.

We have been chosen by God. This great gift we have received from him can fill us with a fearless generosity. To abandon other people, families, or countries because we fear for our own lives is sinful. It is also very tempting. God did create us to survive in this life. But he also created us to trust him even more than we cling to this life. That is why temptation is its most feeble when we are close to God. As Christians, God becomes real life for us. Anything else can become expendable for us if it gets in the way of God's will. But this must be our decision. God has already decided. From the very start, God chose for us. If we do not constantly remind ourselves of the presence of God, the higher goodness we seek in deference to the lesser good tempting us away from God's will become less attractive. But we do have that presence to remember. As Christians, we have the only weapon powerful enough to destroy the power of evil: hope. With hope, we can be obedient to God by working in large or small ways to alleviate poverty or curb or reverse injustice, sustained by that hope we will not be drowned in the despair of the enormity of the problems facing the world. We cannot do these things because we are strong or brave or well spoken. We can do these things because we cling to the promise of salvation and believe that while we are on this earth, we are to work God's will in the world in word and deed. That is why prayer, Bible reading, and fellowship with other Christians are so important. They help us to remember what the will of God is. It is God's will that we be present with those around us by allowing God to be present with us. It is in following our Lord's example that we fearlessly approach evil, not with rage or vengeance but with his word, which speaks to us of his almighty power and mercy. The same almighty power and mercy which give us the courage and the love to work God's will in the world and make it our own.

Lent 4

Life On The Edge Of Faith

A Soldier

The Opening Speech

The Opening Hymn

The Dialogue   Isaiah 40:13-15
Who has held the dust of the earth in a basket,
**Or weighed the mountains on the scales and the hills in
a balance?**
Who has understood the mind of the Lord,
Or instructed him as his counselor?
Whom did the Lord consult to enlighten him,
And who taught him the right way?
Who was it that taught him knowledge
Or showed him the path of understanding?
Surely the nations are like a drop in a bucket;
They are regarded as dust on the scales.

The Old Testament Lesson   Joshua 5:13-15

Psalm 34:4-9   Stanza 1
I sought the Lord, and he answered me;
He delivered me from all my fears.
Those who look to him are radiant;
Their faces are never covered with shame.
This poor man called, and the Lord heard him;
He saved him out of all his troubles.
The angel of the Lord encamps around those who fear him,
And he delivers them.
Taste and see that the Lord is good;
Blessed is the man who takes refuge in him.
Fear the Lord, you his saints,
For those who fear him lack nothing.

41

The Gospel Verse   Matthew 6:19-21

Pastor: Do not store up for yourselves treasures on earth, where
             moth and rust destroy, and where thieves break in and
             steal. But store up for yourselves treasures in heaven,
             where moth and rust do not destroy, and where thieves
             do not break in and steal.

People: **For where your treasure is, there your heart will be
             also.**

The Gospel   Matthew 27:27-31

The Sermon Hymn

Existing on the edge of faith,
Christ's promised peace alone we seek
Grant us the strength to look to you,
We fear our lives are frail and weak.

Praying our lonely way through life
We find temptations cruelly new
Teach us to travel through our lives
Seeking our joy in only you.

Teach us the humble road to walk.
Open our hearts to your embrace
Then we can show the world your love,
With acts of mercy, joy, and grace.

Sermon

Psalm 34:14-18   Stanza 2

Turn from evil and do good;
     Seek peace and pursue it.
The eyes of the Lord are on the righteous
     And his ears are attentive to their cry;
The face of the Lord is against those who do evil,
     To cut off the memory of them from the earth.

The righteous cry out, and the Lord hears them;
He delivers them from all their troubles.
The Lord is close to the brokenhearted
And saves those who are crushed in spirit.

The Offering

The Prayers Of The People
Pastor: Let us pray for the peace and the end of hatred that only
the assurance of our salvation can bring.

During these tumultuous years, Lord, when sabers
are being rattled all over the world, show us the joy and
freedom which come from trusting in you rather than in
military might. Grant to us holy patience so that it is our
life's work to bear witness to your work in the world
and to make way for that work to be felt by people all
over the globe. Waiting on your will,

People: **We pray to you, O Lord.**
Pastor: We pray for all people, especially all of the young people,
who are far from home serving their country's military.
We pray, for their sake that their cause is just. But, Lord,
if their cause is not just, give them what they need to
work to change their government's policies. If that is
not possible, we pray that you help them to find a way
to free themselves from the grip of their cruel govern-
ments. Waiting on your will,

People: **We pray to you, O Lord.**
Pastor: We pray for our own nation's military forces. Keep its
policies just and merciful and keep all its personnel safe.
Waiting on your will,

People: **We pray to you, O Lord.**
Pastor: Standing on the edge of faith, we beg you to hold us up,
dear Lord, with your gift of peace and hear our prayers.
People: **Amen.**

The Lord's Prayer

The Benediction   1 Thessalonians 5:23-24

Pastor: May God himself, the God of peace, sanctify you through and through. May your whole spirit, soul, and body be kept blameless at the coming of our Lord Jesus Christ.

People: **He who calls you is faithful and he will do it.**

The Closing Hymn

Opening Speech: A Soldier

That was the only real excitement I've seen out here in the desert. It is so boring here, you know. I can't wait till I can get back to Italy. Here, nobody speaks our language. They refuse even to learn it, even though if they would just pay attention to the rest of the world, they would see that a new age is dawning. Rome is taking control. This god of theirs is not going to help them. Rome is the only god worth worshiping. Nobody here seems to realize that. Either they hang on to their old religion with their teeth or they just don't know enough to be afraid. I think that's what his problem was, if you want to know the truth.

I suppose that that is what made me so angry. We were saying things that would have made anybody else crazy, and he just stood there and looked at us. He didn't look afraid or sad. He didn't even show how much he must have been hurting. I decided that this guy must have been empty inside. And that really surprised me, because from what I'd heard, he'd caused a lot of trouble up there in Galilee. He had gotten all the natives properly speechified, told them that they would never have to worry about their future and that they would always be free. They were even more stupid than I thought if they bought that. I just bet you that if that guy had just left them alone, they would have come around to Rome's way of thinking. They would have put their kids in Roman schools, and they would have learned to speak Latin and all grown up to be doctors or lawyers. All that guy did was deprive those poor ignorant Jews of the best chance that they ever had.

I think that that is what made me so angry. Because, you know, at bottom, I'm a nice guy. I mean, I don't ordinarily go around hitting prisoners. I don't think a soldier of Rome should take advantage of his position in that way. But, well, everybody else was doing it. And now that I think about it, I have to admit, I didn't really think about anything. I guess I was caught up in the heat of the moment. It makes me feel sort of ashamed now that remember what I was feeling. Because what I was feeling was the kind of gnawing you get when your brother or friend gets to go on a fun trip and you have to stay home and do chores because you'd blown it the week before. Yeah, I think that's what I was feeling. Like this guy had something I needed and I couldn't have it. And the worst of it was that I knew it was my own fault.

Don't ask me how I knew any of this. I just did. And it made me angry. So I hit him and I kept on hitting him. It only made me feel worse. And it doesn't help now that they are saying that this guy didn't stay dead. That he rose and appeared to all of his followers. Part of me keeps wondering if this guy is going to come after me and pay me back for how I treated him, but most of me just wants to see him again.

Lent 4 Sermon

In the early 1980s, and new kind of villain was turning up in pulp fiction. He was very tough and very smart and very beautiful. According to his various creators, these attributes could be traced back to the fact that his parents came from two different races. This gave him the advantage of hybrid vigor, but it also meant that he also was forced to learn to live in two different cultures. This usually left him with a spirit that, because it had been wounded, made for the perfect killing machine. However, for some reason, within five years, this beautiful monster disappeared from the grocery and drugstore shelves. And that made me wonder what made a character that at one time was so compelling he was showing up in every pulp writer's collection so unpleasant that readers all over the country rejected him. Maybe this monster is too upsetting for us, and perhaps, he hits too close to home.

To be able to discern the different sources of authority in life is one of the signs of maturity. Maybe this particular villain evolved because of the average human being's own struggle to declare allegiance and identify priorities.

It is clear from the story of our Lord's suffering and death that this is not a new problem. It is always the case that it is necessary for us to give up or at least lessen our allegiance to one goal or person in order to pledge such loyalty to another. This nearly always causes distress. But it seems odd that we would be talking about such a thing regarding our Lord's sacrifice for us. Shouldn't such a manifestation clear away all competition for devotion? When we are completely aware of our true situation, there is nothing on earth that could tempt us away from devoting all our allegiance to God and even more important, placing all of our hope in the salvation he has promised us. But sometimes, we run into trouble doing that. Things get in our way. Sometimes, very often, in fact, what gets in our way is the simple pleasure of living.

There is a very old story about a man who visited his lady friend every Wednesday evening. This went on for some number of years. Eventually the lady began to wonder if her gentleman friend was ever going to ask her to marry him. So, she brought it up herself. He said that he was hardly opposed to the idea of marriage, but the only problem was that, what would he do on Wednesday nights? That may seem like a story which gently expresses how we cheat ourselves of the best by clinging to the second best. But the truth of it is that eventually, that man will find himself alone and afraid on a Tuesday morning or a Saturday afternoon.

We will not accept the best until we realize that we cannot pay for it and that that is all right. But until we come to that realization, we will struggle to defend, and if necessary, fight to protect our right to embrace the second best as our god and the second best will eventually abandon us as Rome would eventually abandon that soldier, if only at death. But our God will not abandon us, particularly not at death. But do you know what that means? That means that this side of heaven, we are free to embrace all of the beauty and power and wonder of God's world, not as our gods, but as partners in our service to God. This ends our anger and our fear and opens us the limitless possibilities God has for us here on earth as well as in heaven.

A musical composer said that the most important thing in the world to do is to remember that no matter what you do, someone else has already done it before. He knew that he could never consider a tune or a phrase of music that had not already been considered, and probably written down, by some other composer. This notion did not fill him with despair, causing him to think that it was not worth trying anything new because no matter what he tried, it had been done before. Rather, he said that it had the opposite effect on him, especially with regard to his musical composition. Because everything had already been done, he could relax about trying to be the first one to do something. He was free to write anything that came to him. This theory opened to him many possibilities. In embracing the Savior of Calvary as our God, we admit that everything has been done before and we open for ourselves limitless possibilities.

Life On The Edge Of Faith

A City Dweller

Opening Speech

Opening Hymn

The Dialogue   Hosea 14:1-2

Return, O Israel, to the Lord your God.
Your sins have been your downfall!
Take words with you
And return to the Lord.
Say to him: Forgive all our sins and receive us graciously,
That we may offer the fruit of our lips.

The Old Testament Lesson   Deuteronomy 21:22-23

Psalm 130:1-4

Out of the depths I cry to you, O Lord; O Lord, hear my voice.
Let your ears be attentive to my cry for mercy.
If you, O Lord, kept a record of sins,
O Lord, who could stand?
But with you there is forgiveness;
Therefore you are feared.

The Gospel Verse   Matthew 6:19-21
Pastor: Do not store up for yourselves treasures on earth, where
             moth and rust destroy, and where thieves break in and
             steal. But store up for yourselves treasures in heaven,
             where moth and rust do not destroy, and where thieves
             do not break in and steal.
People: **For where your treasure is, there your heart will be
             also.**

The Gospel   Matthew 27:32-44

The Sermon Hymn   "Existing On The Edge Of Faith"
Existing on the edge of faith,
Christ's promised peace alone we seek
Grant us the strength to look to you,
We fear our lives are frail and weak.

Loneliness lies in wait for us
When in our walk we stray from you
Help us to watch your loving will
Fill our exhausted lives anew.

Teach us the humble road to walk.
Open our hearts to your embrace
Then we can show the world your love,
With acts of mercy, joy, and grace.

The Sermon

Psalm 130:4-8
I wait for the Lord, my soul waits,
    And in his word I put my hope.
My soul waits for the Lord more than watchmen wait for the
morning,
    More than watchmen wait for the morning.
O Israel, put your hope in the Lord,
    For with the Lord is unfailing love
And with him is full redemption.
    He himself will redeem Israel from all their sins.

The Offering

The Prayers Of The People
Pastor: Let us pray to show the world the miracle of God's love.
        Dear God, we give you thanks that you have cre-
        ated us to be people who reach out to each other. Help
        us daily to recognize that joyful reality. Just as impor-
        tantly, as your people, help us to show that joy to others.

There are so many people who live lives isolated from you, from other people, and even from themselves. We give you thanks, Lord, that as we show to the world the joy of fellowship, we also show it the power of forgiveness. Looking to you for all our hope,

People: **We pray to you, O Lord.**

Pastor: Bring into clear focus our world's need for your love and give us the courage to share it. So often, we find it easier to cut ourselves off from those in need because we find their situations distressing and because we remember times in our own lives where we have had to struggle through our own difficult circumstances and we do not remember anyone giving us a hand out. Remind us, Lord, that without you and your love, our situations would indeed be desperate, and that not only did your Son give us a hand. He gave up his whole body so that we might be rescued from that desperate situation. Looking to you for all our hope,

People: **We pray to you, O Lord.**

Pastor: As we near the observation of your son's sacrifice, fill us not only with the knowledge of our sin, but, more importantly, with the knowledge of your Son's forgiving grace. Looking to you for all our hope,

People: **We pray to you, O Lord.**

Pastor: Standing on the edge of faith, we beg you to hold us up, dear Lord, with your gift of peace and hear our prayers.

People: **Amen.**

The Lord's Prayer

The Benediction   1 Thessalonians 5:23-24

Pastor: May God himself, the God of peace, sanctify you through and through. May your whole spirit, soul, and body be kept blameless at the coming of our Lord Jesus Christ.

People: **He who calls you is faithful and he will do it.**

The Closing Hymn

51

Opening Speech: City Dweller

Well, I hope the place will quiet down now. All this talk about miracles and Messiah was getting to me. I can't say that I ever really paid too much attention to him until now. Of course, I heard all about him. He was the only thing anybody was talking about. It seemed like everyone I talked to knew someone who knew someone who had been healed by him. Urban legends are so entertaining. And occasionally, I did find this pathetic scenario grimly amusing, but I guess, most of the time I just thought it was sad. I think of all of those people who place their faith and hope in one trickster or another just to have them take off with the collection or the wife of one of the members. At least this one didn't let them down that way. But it amounted to pretty much the same thing, don't you think? Another blowhard with a bag of tricks who couldn't deliver what he promised. He promised all of these things, promises that we have heard over and over again: peace, freedom, independence. And what made it so very ridiculous is that he claimed to be the Messiah, the Son of God. If he was God, why did he die? And you know, it wasn't like he was the first healer we'd ever seen wave a stick either.

Although, and now this is the problem, this guy seemed to break every rule you go by to trap a trickster. Most of these scum cure lame and blind people that nobody has ever seen before and no one ever sees again. This one cured the beggars that everybody knew. Beggars that I knew. One particular blind beggar that I knew. That really gets me. I just wish he had stayed out of my life. I'm not mean. I'm glad the poor fellow can see now, but I guess you don't realize how much you count on consistency until it's gone. It used to be that every morning, on my way to the office, I would see him sitting there with his cup. Now, every morning, even though I know he won't be there, I still look for him. And when he's not there I remember why, and I get scared. And everybody else seems to think that is so wonderful. Don't they understand what this means? It means that rules no longer mean anything. It means that you can't count on the things you used to think wouldn't and couldn't be challenged. Everybody has a certain path this life has given them to travel. Some are harder than others. Like I say, I am glad that beggar's path was shifted, that his hard life was made more livable. But it scares me to think that his life was changed in that way at all. If that man gave him his eyesight back, that means that there is a strange power at work in the world. And if there really is an unearthly force at work in the world, then what good is all of our work and planning? If at anytime, even this simple man from the country can snap his fingers and someone regains his sight, anybody could just as easily snap his fingers and somebody could go blind. I'm not sure I want any other human being having that much control over me. The only way I can even bear to think about it is to imagine that he might just have been the Messiah, the Son of God, and that his goodness is real. How he might be the one to bring peace and freedom and independence. But then I think of how he died. All I know is that I sure wish that things would calm down.

Lent 5 Sermon

In 1986, a woman living in San Antonio, Texas, was diagnosed as having the AIDS virus after she received an infected blood transfusion. Eight years later, she took another AIDS test with a false name and discovered that a terrible mistake had been made and that she had never had the virus. This might have made her happy. But during those eight years, she had spent much time, energy, and money on cures. She was subjected to the terrible and exhausting side effects of drugs which were never necessary and, as an outgrowth of this, she watched her two sons' fear and despair turn into anger and their change from rage to alienation and finally to desertion. She heard the good news too late.

Jesus died to give us the good news. We had the virus of sin. His death took away sin's power to harm us. But when we do not accept that good news, we behave, much like the woman whose story I just told. We spend all of this energy trying to achieve immortality or happiness or just peace while we are laboring under this heavy load which Jesus died to remove from us. It sometimes seems that we are desperate to keep the load of our sin, as if that sin makes us who we are more than the positive aspects of our personalities, as though we want to hang onto the very thing that makes us sick. In so doing, we reject the one thing that will make us well.

There is a story about two members of a congregation: one of them was very young and the other one was very old. George was quite unique. For fifty years, the people who went into his store left knowing that they were somebody special. George had a gift for mirror writing which he used to make people feel good whenever he met someone, especially a young person, for the first time. George wrote the person's name down twice at the same time. He would write the name with his right hand so it could be read. At the same time, he would write the name backwards with his left hand, so that when the person got home, he could hold that piece of paper up to the mirror and he could read it. In this congregation there was also a young father named Joe who was distressed to discover his son writing his name backwards and then running and holding the piece of paper up to a mirror and reading it that way. This young father was distressed and tried to get his son to stop doing that because he had read in some book that mirror writing was a common manifestation of dyslexia. Well, apparently, George hadn't read that book. No one ever told him that the gift he had given to three generations of children was caused by a learning disability. But, George was unique. If somebody had told him, it's doubtful that he would have cared. He did not fear his strange gift. He embraced it, but what made it even more special was that he embraced it not only for his own enjoyment, but even more so for the enjoyment of others.

We have a story to share with others. Our Lord died on the cross to pay the debt of our sin, but because he died in this way at the hand of human beings, other human beings have told this story. Therefore, when there are those around us who have forgotten this good news, we can share it. It may seem to some of them unbelievable, often because the news does not appear to have anything to do with them. They feel that they have found their heaven on earth. It may take a terrible loss for them to embrace this good news. But to most others it will be hard to believe because it is simply too good to believe. Someone must remind them. God has given us this privilege: to remind the people of the world that they are free from their fear of death.

Life On The Edge Of Faith

Maundy Thursday Worship Service

The Opening Hymn

The Opening Litany   Isaiah 65:17-20, 24
Behold, I will create new heavens and a new earth. The former
things will not be remembered,
   Nor will they come to mind.
But be glad and rejoice forever in what I will create,
   **For I will create Jerusalem to be a delight and its people
   a joy.**
I will rejoice over Jerusalem and take delight in my people;
   **The sound of weeping and of crying will be heard in it
   no more.**
Before they call I will answer;
   While they are still speaking I will hear.
The wolf and the lamb will feed together,
   And the lion will eat straw like the ox.

The First Reading   Exodus 12:1-14

The Imposition Of Ashes

The Service Of Public Confession And Absolution
Pastor: From the first day of Lent, when we felt the filth of
               the ashes placed on our foreheads, we have allowed
               the awareness of our sin to grow. Throughout these
               six weeks, as that comprehension grew, so did our
               horror at our own alienation from each other and
               from God. But even as our understanding of our sepa-
               ration grew, our understanding of our personal need

for God increased. And it was during these past six weeks that we remembered that, even while we were in awe of our own weakness and immorality, God is with us and has redeemed us.

People: **In coming here this evening, we declare to God, to the world, and to each other our need for forgiveness. To have the courage to make such a declaration, we have not only faced our sins and called them by their right names, we have realized that God has the only way for us out of our trap, a trap which we ourselves set, again and again, by means of our sin.**

Pastor: Therefore, let us confess our sins to each other and to God and hear his word of forgiveness.

People: **Though we are unworthy, you have forgiven us, Lord**

Right Side: **When we fail to bring your love into consideration or when we slip into apathy or despair about the world,**

Left side: **When we fail to take strength and courage from the example of your Son,**

People: **Though we are unworthy, you have forgiven us, Lord.**

Right Side: **When by our inaction, we allow injustice, greed, selfishness, and even cruelty to go unchecked,**

Left Side: **When by our inaction, we allow your truth to go unspoken and undefended, ignored, and mocked,**

People: **Though we are unworthy, you have forgiven us, Lord.**

Right Side: **When with our apathy and despair, we fall into dangerous, abusive, and destructive habits,**

Left Side: **Or allow our hopelessness to turn into cynicism and the base desire for power, wealth, or other forms of earthly corruptible security,**

People: **Though we are unworthy, you have forgiven us, Lord.**

Right Side:	When in our weakness and fear, we allow ourselves to be dragged down into a place in which we see no way to live which does not involve sinful behavior,
Left Side:	And perhaps find our strength and our courage in sin instead of your goodness,
People:	Though we are unworthy, you have forgiven us, Lord.
Right Side:	When we find profane power and treacherous security in acts of injustice, greed, selfishness, and cruelty,
Left Side:	And allow others to pay the cost for that power and security,
People:	Though we are unworthy, you have forgiven us, Lord.
Right Side:	When we neglect the truth which your Son died to show us, when we abuse those who try to spread that truth with words and actions with our fearful doubt and our lack of support,
Left Side:	When we show the world how little your love really means to us,
People:	Though we are unworthy, you have forgiven us, Lord.
Pastor:	We lay our lives, unworthy of even a glance from you, at your feet, knowing that we will receive your mercy, not because anything we have done or can hope to do but because of your Son's sacrifice which paid our debt.
People:	Humbly, we give you thanks. Amen.

The Gospel Verse   Matthew 6:19-21

Pastor:	Do not store up for yourselves treasures on earth, where moth and rust destroy, and where thieves break in and steal. But store up for yourselves treasures in heaven, where moth and rust do not destroy, and where thieves do not break in and steal.
People:	For where your treasure is, there your heart will be also.

The Gospel Lesson   Matthew 26:17-29

The Sermon Hymn   "Existing On The Edge Of Faith"
Existing on the edge of faith,
Christ's promised peace alone we seek
Grant us the strength to look at you,
We fear our lives are frail and weak.

Our hearts are opened to your love
When we remember our dear Lord
And his giving over life for us
Our peace forever to afford.

Teach us the humble road to walk.
Open our hearts to your embrace
Then we can show the world your love,
With acts of mercy, joy, and grace.

The Sermon

The Prayers Of The People
Pastor: Let us pray to be open to our Lord's mercy.
              As we near the end of our Lenten journey, Lord, we
              hanker more and more for the announcement of your
              Son's resurrection. We know the bitterness our sin has
              caused us and how it has kept us from embracing the
              freedom you meant for us to have. Fill our hearts with
              the knowledge of your forgiveness, Lord, so that we may
              rejoice in forgiving ourselves and each other. Our heads
              deeply bowed,
People: **We pray to you, O Lord.**
Pastor: As we prepare to celebrate your Son's resurrection, cause
              us to remember not only our own temptation to exist on
              the edge of faith and not roam in its wondrous opportu-
              nity, but also keep us mindful of those who are still un-
              aware of the freedom that could be theirs. There are so
              many, Lord, who know your name but know nothing of

your love. Give us the courage to show them that love and, as a result, free us to feel the joy that comes from it. Our heads deeply bowed,

People: **We pray to you, O Lord.**

Pastor: We give you thanks, dear Father, that you sent your Son to be among us. We also give you thanks that he presented us with the loving mandate of Holy Communion. By means of this action, we see the blessings of both salvation and community. Our heads deeply bowed,

People: **We pray to you, O Lord.**

Pastor: Standing on the edge of faith, we beg you to hold us up, dear Lord, with your gift of peace and hear our prayers.

People: **Amen.**

The Offering

Psalm 51

Have mercy on me, O God, according to your unfailing love;
According to your great compassion blot out my transgressions.
Wash away all my iniquity and cleanse me from my sin.
For I know my transgressions, and my sin is always before me.
Against you, you only, have I sinned
And done what is evil in your sight,
So that you are proved right when you speak
And justified when you judge.
Surely I was sinful at birth,
Sinful from the time my mother conceived me.
Surely you desire truth in the inner parts;
You teach me wisdom in the inmost place.
Cleanse me with hyssop, and I will be clean;
Wash me, and I will be whiter than snow.
Let me hear joy and gladness;
Let the bones you have crushed rejoice.
Hide your face from my sins
And blot out all my iniquity.

Create in me a pure heart, O God,
And renew a steadfast spirit within me.
Do not cast me from your presence
Or take your Holy Spirit from me.
Restore to me the joy of your salvation
And grant me a willing spirit, to sustain me.
Then I will teach transgressors your ways,
And sinners will turn back to you.
Save me from bloodguilt, O God, the God who saves me,
And my tongue will sing of your righteousness.
O Lord, open my lips,
And my mouth will declare your praise.
You do not delight in sacrifice, or I would bring it;
You do not take pleasure in burnt offerings.
The sacrifices of God are a broken spirit;
A broken and contrite heart, O God, you will not despise.
In your good pleasure make Zion prosper;
Build up the walls of Jerusalem.
Then there will be righteous sacrifices, whole burnt offerings to delight you;
Then bulls will be offered on your altar.

The Word Of Institution For Maundy Thursday

Pastor: Great God in Heaven, you sent your Son to take on our condition and, being sinless, to die for our sin. Raising him from death, you sent your Spirit to help us to understand things that are too beautiful for us even to see. We give you thanks for these beautiful and incomprehensible things which free us from fear and free us for service. Break us free from our chains, Lord, and bind us to your will, which your Son so humbly obeyed.

In the night in which he was betrayed, our Lord Jesus took bread and gave thanks, broke it and gave it to his disciples saying: "Take and eat; this is my body, given for you. Do this for the remembrance of me." Again, after supper, he took the cup, gave thanks, and gave it for all to drink saying: "This cup is the new covenant in my blood, shed for you and for all people for the forgiveness of sin. Do this for the remembrance of me."

The Lord's Prayer

The Prayer After Communion

Pastor: We give you thanks, Lord, that you have welcomed us, unworthy as we are, into your presence. Fill us with a gratitude born of the knowledge of your Son's sacrifice and send us forth to come to embrace the freedom and joy this sacrifice brings.

People: Amen.

(If the Altar is stripped after Holy Communion, Psalm 22 may be sung or said.)

The Closing Hymn

Maundy Thursday Sermon

Our God is all love. Our God is all powerful. Our God is all knowing. Our God is all understanding. But one thing our God is not is well-mannered. He told people to gobble their food. As the leader of the group, he does the work of the slave. Both of these things brought gasps of disapproval from those who first heard them. But we thank God that he did them both. We cannot read the story of the first Passover without feeling the anxiety of those Hebrew slaves who, after 400 years, were finally experiencing the possibility of freedom. And there is no clearer message of the assurance of belonging than for a master to do the work of a servant as our Lord did by washing his apostles' feet.

In these two strange and offensive commands, our Lord reminds us that most often his will and the will of the world look entirely different, but that his will reflects the reality of grace and compassion found in him and in us as a gift from him. His will abolishes the earthly law which states for every winner, there must be a loser. When we look at the story of the first Passover, we see people whose attention is justifiably fixed on the danger of the situation. In short order, death will literally surround them by means of the inexorable hand of God himself. Shortly after that, they will have to deal with Pharaoh's bloody hand because Pharaoh definitely believed that for every winner there was a loser.

This story reminds us that ours is a world filled with danger and temptation, and that it is moving away from God and not toward him. To remain near God, even though God is never far from us, we must constantly resist the tide of sin and temptation that we will face in the world. Even after our Lord's death and resurrection this remains true. In fact, it is even more true because having embraced the good news our Lord died to bring us, we live a life that is moving in the opposite direction of the rest of the world. Although we now see that in Christ there are no losers, we live, pray, and work in a world that does not understand that freeing truth.

Therefore as Christians, it may, at times, seem as though we must take in as much spiritual nourishment as quickly as we can to keep from being swept away in the tide of the world, as though we were being told to gobble our food as the ancient Hebrews were. Moving in the opposite direction from the world is a lot of work. But it is because we are moving in the opposite direction from the world that we know what true living really is.

An adventurer decided to take his family along with him once. In order to convince his family to keep up with him, he would say, "We are moving upstream. Only dead things move downstream. Living things move upstream." We are moving upstream. Because that is true, we know that we are truly alive. We are assured of our belonging to God. We can afford to be a servant. We do not have to constantly demand guarantees that our position is secure.

An old *Twilight Zone* episode featured a robot baseball pitcher who could strike out anybody. The other teams became suspicious and demanded a physical exam. The robot's creators, realizing that he would have no pulse, quickly installed a heart in the robot's chest. The robot passed the physical exam and returned to the playing field. However, with his new heart he would no longer strike out anybody. It seems that the robot baseball player had made a discovery. With his new heart, he realized that he no longer had to be the master of all he surveyed in order to be happy.

That is what the Christian understands. The Christian knows that belonging to God, all victories are unnecessary. God through Christ has won the battle for us.

Good Friday

Life On The Edge Of Faith

Good Friday Worship Service

Pastor: Let us pray.
People: **Lord Jesus, you carried our sins in your own body
onto the tree so that we might have life. May we and
all who remember this day find new life in you now
and in the world to come, where you live and reign
with the Father and the Holy Spirit, now and forever. Amen.**

The Hymn   "O Sacred Head" (vv. 1 and 2)

The First Reading   Genesis 3:17-21

Pastor: Let us pray. Dear Father in heaven, grant to all who look
to you this night the assurance that only comes from
your total victory over evil. Fill us, Lord, with this life-
healing peace. We come before you at the invitation of
your Son.
People: **In his name we pray.**

(Extinguish the first candle)

Meditation
    Concluding his address to the Kennedy School of Social Policy
regarding the past and the possible future of the Social Security
Administration, veteran Senator Daniel P. Moynihan advised the
young people gathered in the room that unless they had thirty years
to devote to it, they should not even think about careers in social
policy. He apparently understood very well that getting the right
answers was no big achievement. The real challenge was asking
the right questions. The answer comes in meeting need with solution. This takes understanding the options and the sources. But don't

67

even waste your time rooting those out until you know the right questions to ask. It is obvious that Adam and Eve did not know the right questions to ask, because while they found a solution which may have seemed expedient, it left them literally out in the cold. It seemed to God that he would have to teach them what question they should be asking. They had to discover how hard life really could be, how ill-equipped they were to handle it on their own, how they, sooner than later, would need God. In this first of many great acts of mercy, God pushed Adam and Eve out into the real world. We must pray to be pushed into that real world. We make our own Edens out of false dreams and cheap thrills, but God is always near us when sin eventually does what it does best: make us miserable and thus pushes us out of the garden of our own sin.

The Hymn   "Rock Of Ages, Cleft For Me"

The Second Reading   Genesis 22:10-14

The Sermon Hymn   "Existing On The Edge Of Faith"
Existing on the edge of faith,
Christ's promised peace alone we seek
Grant us the strength to look to you,
We fear our lives are frail and weak.

Treating your son with low regard
It is our death to which we cling.
Why do we worship ancient waste
When he has come to be our king?

Teach us the humble road to walk.
Open our hearts to your embrace
Then we can show the world your love,
With acts of mercy, joy, and grace.

Pastor: Let us pray. Dear Father in heaven, grant to all who look to you this night the freedom which grows out of the assurance of our redemption. Fill us, Lord, with your vision of our future. We come before you at the invitation of your Son.

People: In his name we pray. Amen.

(*Extinguish the second candle*)

Meditation

No matter where we are in our spiritual lives, we will regularly find ourselves exisiting on the edge of faith. Our sin will occasionally drive us back into the hole of our sin but God's grace will always be present to invite us to frolic joyfully through the terrain of faith's freedom. When we slip back into the hole of our sin, we allow ourselves to forget that there is a terrible problem and that, on our own, we cannot hope to find the answers. When we are living the life of faith's freedom, we know that there are questions to be answered, but we leave both the questions and the answers to God, finding all we need in his presence. It is while we are existing on the edge of faith that we are seeking those questions because we know that until we find them, we cannot hope of ever finding a way to secure our lives. Perhaps God is nudging Abraham out of his garden of family security. While family is a gift from God, it is as able to be the object of our idolatry as anything else. In the horror of Abraham's obedience, he found his true security. That security was not that no matter what, God would never allow his son to die. It was that he knew that somehow God himself would provide the sacrifice which would provide the answer to the question we are seeking.

The Third Reading   Isaiah 11:1-3, 6-9

The Hymn   "In The Cross Of Christ I Glory"

Pastor: Let us pray. Dear Father in heaven, grant to all who look to you this night the courage to which freedom gives birth. Fill us, Lord, with your sense of justice. We come before you at the invitation of your Son.

People: In his name we pray. Amen.

(*Extinguish the third candle*)

Meditation

Even though it is true that when we sin, we slip into a hole filled with sin, we can delude ourselves into believing that it is a garden. That is why we need to be forced from the security of its borders. But sometimes, when we think that we are in pursuit of God's will we can forget that it is God who created us and sustains us and loved us enough to become a human being and die for us. Therefore, we do need to remind ourselves that God did not send his Son to take on our sin and to make life merely possible for us, but joyful for us. But we continue to struggle against it. There is a story of an American tourist who is in India on the day of a pilgrimage to the top of a sacred mountain. During the day, thousands of people climbed the steep path to the mountaintop. The tourist, who believed himself to be in good physical shape, decided to share in the experience. But within a half hour, he found himself to be out of breath and unable to climb another step, while women carrying babies, and frail old men with canes, moved easily past him up the hill. The man said: "I don't understand it. How can those people do it when I cannot?" His Indian friend answered: "It is because you have the typical American habit of seeing everything as a test. You see the mountain as your enemy and you set out to defeat it. So naturally, the mountain fights back and it is stronger than you are. We do not see the mountain as our enemy to be conquered. The purpose of our climb is to become one with the mountain and so it lifts us up and carries us along." Our Lord and Savior with all of his gifts, has come to us to carry us home with him.

The Fourth Reading   Matthew 1:20-23

The Hymn   "O Sacred Head" (vv. 3 and 4)

Pastor: Let us pray. Dear Father in heaven, grant to all who look to you this night the faithful joy that fills us up and spills out into the world. Fill us, Lord, with the desire to touch

all with your love. We come before you at the invitation
of your Son.

People: **In his name we pray. Amen.**

(*Extinguish the fourth candle*)

Meditation

Lately, the image of a famine stricken land is so commonplace
it is no longer newsworthy, but unforunately famines are still killing children and threatening futures. What makes it even more tragic
is the fact that civil war and the resulting breakdown of law and
society cause famine more readily than drought or insect plague.
In the early 1990s, horrifying images came from the tiny African
country of Somalia. The combination of drought, civil war, and the
complete breakdown of law and order rendered Somalia a country
in which life was nearly impossible and starvation was commonplace. Relief, desperately needed, was either stolen by bandits or
used as a bargaining chip by one of the many opposing forces before it could reach those so critically in need. And of the many
terrible things that were going on in that community, among the
most frustrating was the fact that the news media portrayed the
situation as though there was no possible solution in sight. However, I listened to one radio broadcast on which a relief worker said
that the only possible situation would be for the U.N. to so flood
the country with food that the bandits could not physically steal it
all and that it was no longer a viable bargaining tool. Make food
food again, and not a weapon of cruelty. That's what our Lord did
by coming to earth. He drowned sin with his blood. He snuffed sin
out with his righteousness and brought forgiveness to the earth.

The Final Reading   Luke 23:44-49

The Lord's Prayer

The Hymn   "Were You There? (vv. 1-3)

(*Extinguish the last candle*)

(*The congregation will leave in silence.*)